The Seven Types of Water for Purification

A **GREENFIG** Book

Written By
Fatimah Ghandour

Illustrated By

CHY Illustration & Design

Name

_____

Publisher: Green Fig
Pennsylvania, USA
www.gogreenfig.com

Green Fig

Dear Parents & Educators

Teaching children to pray is a milestone in the life of Muslim parents. Prayer is an integral of Islam and a pillar of the Religion. The key to prayer is purification. Allāh, The Almighty, praised those who make purification in the Qur'ān.

$$﴿ إِنَّ اللَّهَ يُحِبُّ التَّوَّابِينَ وَيُحِبُّ الْمُتَطَهِّرِينَ ﴾$$

سورة البقرة/222

The Prophet ﷺ said, "الطُّهور شَطْرُ الإيمان" narrated by Muslim. This hadeeth means to take care of one's purification is like half of Iman, i.e. it is a great matter in the Religion. If one's purification is invalid, one's prayer, which is the best deed after believing in Allāh and his messenger, is invalid too. Knowing the judgments related to purification is a necessary matter that a Muslim needs all the time. Teaching children the matters of purification such as wudu', ghusl, and removing najas filthy material is consequently very important.

The Seven Types of Water for Purification is the first book published in the Purification and Prayer series by Green Fig. It serves an educational tool to teach kids and students the judgments related to the seven types of pure and purifying water that one can use for wudu' in accordance with authentic fiqh texts such as The Text of Abu Shuja' in the Shafii school. It also teaches children, in its fun and engaging format, facts about water, a ubiquitous element in their everyday life in addition to many other religious benefits.

Take great care in nurturing skills in your children to perfect an action that is very essential in this life and of great consequence in the next life in the Hereafter. Teaching children how to make purification and prayer is like sowing seeds for everlasting happiness!

We will be happy to hear from you at info@gogreenfig.com

Green Fig Team

Water is the first creation and is the origin of the other creations in this universe, living and non-living. The Prophet ﷺ said that God created everything from water.

"إنّ اللهَ تعالى خلَق كُلَّ شيءٍ مِنَ الماء."

It is mentioned in the Qur'ān!

﴿وجعَلنا مِنَ الماءِ كُلَّ شَىءٍ حَيٍّ﴾*

سورة الأنبياء / 30

The meaning of this verse is that God created all things, whether living or non-living, from water. The living things were mentioned in this ayah for their honor over the non-living things.

Allāh is the Creator; He created everything. This means Allāh has no beginning and everything else has a beginning. Allāh existed in eternity and nothing else existed: no water, no place, no earth, no skies, no space, no animals, no angels, and no humans. The first thing that God created was water. From this original water, Allāh created everything else. Allāh created the second creation, The Throne (Al-'Arsh), from water. The Throne's place was above this water. It was floating above the water. After a period of time, water and Al-'Arsh became separated by a distance. This original water is now in the upper world. From there, water descends to earth in the lower world, but the attributes of water change when it reaches our earth.

Water is, indeed, a great blessing, and we are surrounded by it. We use it every day for drinking, making wudu', cleaning ourselves, and many more things. The source of water comes in many different shapes and forms...

But which type of water can we make wudu' with? Wudu' is a purification, so you can make wudu' from any pure and purifying water. There are seven types of water we can use for wudu'. Are you ready to go over them? Let's go!

Rain Water

It comes directly from the sky. Catch some when it rains. Splash it on you. It is good.

Have you experienced water suddenly coming down like a shower? That's called rain water. It can water your flowers and plants, as well as cleanse the ground and give the air a breeze.

Smell it, when it rains. Feel it, or even make wudu' with it.

Save it, collect it, and use it later. Wash your bike on a sunny day. Water your plants if the rain goes away.

Catch it where it falls, play with your brother or sister under those fun, fun drops.

Fill up your swimming pool, wouldn't that be cool?

Do you see how rain water is helpful, in many, many things? It is a blessing, for sure.

Sea Water

Take just a little bit of water from the big ocean to make wudu'! The sea surely is a vast place, filled with so much water, so salty you can't drink. How amazing can it be, to see the raindrops falling into the sea. You can visit the ocean and make wudu' there, while watching the beautiful waves, coming out and back into the beautiful sea.

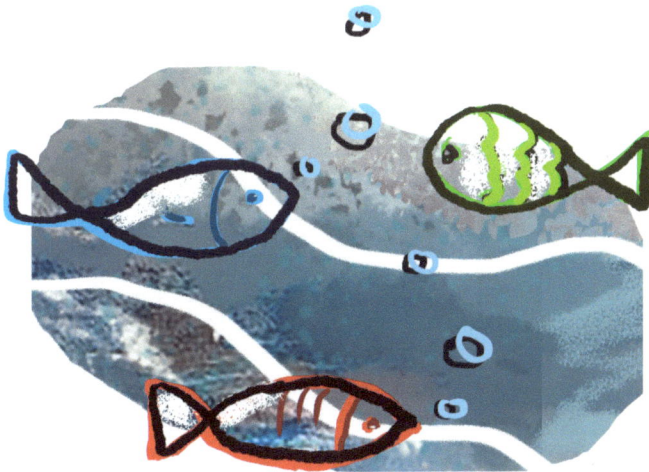

River Water

Run along the zigzag river. Look at the running streams, creeks, and lakes.

Even if you live far away from a river, you can see its water at home. Just turn on the tap, and there it is! We use it in the shower, kitchen, or even outdoor.

You can play with it, on a hot day, or even help your mom and dad with the dishes!

The river's streams are long and smooth flowing. Some of those pleasant streams fall into the bay or ocean.

Well Water

I say '"water". I hear back "water" echoing from the well. I drop a pebble and I hear the splash. Well water is deep, underground water. If you visit a farm, you can pump the water in a well, and just see how it comes out. A very special well is called Zamzam in Mecca. The water of zamzam is a blessed water. It is the best water we can get nowadays.

Spring Water

The water we drink from springs is another form of water.

Have you ever been hiking and saw water springing from the ground or between the rocks? Or maybe you swam in a pool of water from a spring? Even if you never saw one, you probably had some when you felt thirsty and drank from a refreshing bottled water. This water is called spring water and is pure and purifying, for sure.

It comes all the way from those big beautiful mountains and valleys, you see.

Snow Water

Fluffy and white, later melting into pure water.

It starts off gorgeously white. It covers the trees, streets, bushes, and homes and makes a beautiful scene. Go ahead make some snowballs, freeze them, and take them out in the summer. Its water is icy cold, but, like the other types, greatly benefits us.

Hail Water

Tic tac the sound hail makes. Now, this is something you would want to see! It comes in so many sizes; light, heavy, big, and small. Some are like little drops, or pebbles, while others are like a stone. Yet, it is a blessing, truly. A form of water we can use when hail melts. Surely pure and purifying!

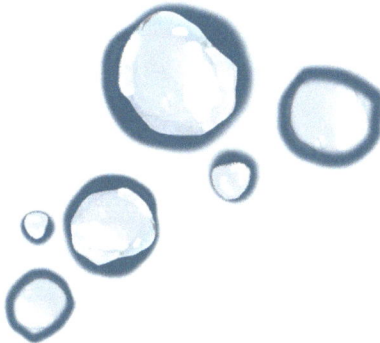

So, go out and explore all these wonderful types of water. Make wudu' from any of them that you choose. Or, even try them all, you have nothing to lose. Fill up a bucket, and name it what you choose. Rain, spring, sea, river, well, hail, or snow water, they're all pure, and purifying. Explore and be thankful; they're all blessings that we are surrounded by.

RAIN

WELL

SEA

SPRING

SNOW

HAIL

RIVER

But do you know what is the best type of water? It is the water that sprang from between the fingers of our Prophet Mu<u>h</u>ammad, may peace be upon him. Hundreds of companions who were there drank from it and made wudu' with this water.

It was a great miracle!

The Blessed Water of Zamzam

Zamzam water appeared at the time of Prophet Abraham, may peace be upon him. He took his son Isma'il and Isma'il's mother, Hajar, to Makkah. Isma'il was still a nursing baby. At that time, Makkah did not have people living in it, nor did it have any plants or water. The kaabah was also destroyed by the flood that happened at the time of Prophet Noah. When the water and dates that were with Lady Hajar ran out, she and her son became very thirsty and hungry. Angel Gabriel appeared and hit the ground with his wing and water sprang out! This water became known as Zamzam. The well of Zamzam is located near the kaabah. Nowadays, all the pilgrims who go to Hajj bring bottles of Zamzam water back home with them. Don't miss the opportunity to drink from it; it has so many benefits!

Rivers from Paradise!

Did you know that four rivers have their origin in Paradise before they enter the earth in a place and a manner not known to us and spring in a different place on earth?
The four rivers are: the Nile, the Euphrates, Sayhan and Jayhan. The last two rivers are in the region of Turkey.
The Prophet said."

"سَيْحَان وجَيْحَان والنِّيلُ والفُراتُ كُلٌّ مِن أنهارِ الجنَّةِ"

Narrated by Al-Bukhariyy, Muslim, and Ahmad in his Musnad.

One of these four rivers is also considered historically to be the longest river in the world. Which one is that?

Yara Mahdi was a ten-year-old girl when she began her artistic journey through a collaborative project with Green Fig. She has always excelled in the art of illustrating, brush strokes, and blending colors. She is currently a graduate student at the Lebanese University, majoring in Fine Arts. Her passion has led her to establish **CHY Illustration & Design** in collaboration with her father, which focuses on illustrations for children's books and books' design.

Green Fig

Green Fig is a publishing house that specializes in Religious books, stories and a variety of educational material for children, teens, parents, and teachers. Green Fig resources serve as a means to nurture children with values that will promote their growth into responsible good-loving individuals. Green Fig satisfies the curious mind with meticulously curated content that flows smoothly in a logical sequence.

Green Fig takes pride of its special contribution to bring to the modern reader, especially the young ones, the concepts present in the classical authentic texts of the beautiful and moderate religion of Islam in a clear language and format they understand and love. Like a fresh exhilarating breeze, Green Fig smartly designed and conceptualized books intertwined with a precious content, take the reader into a journey where the desired aim is to get closer and closer to "living happily ever after"!

Encourage your child to memorize:

"The types of water that are valid to use in purification are seven: rainwater, sea water, river water, well water, spring water, melted snow, and melted hail. "

From The text of Abu Shuja'

"الْمِياهُ الَّتِي يَجوزُ بِها التَّظهيرُ سَبْعُ مِياهٍ: ماءُ السَّماءِ وماءُ البَحْرِ وماءُ النَّهْرِ وماءُ البِئْرِ وماءُ العَيْنِ وماءُ الثَّلْجِ وماءُ البَرَدِ."

كتاب الطهارة - متن أبي شُجاع